The Film

Its Use In Popular Education

By

M. Jackson-Wrigley

Double 9 BOOKS

The Film
Its Use In Popular Education
by M. Jackson-Wrigley

ISBN: 978-93-61429-12-5

Published by

DOUBLE 9 BOOKS

2/13-B, Ansari Road
Daryaganj, New Delhi – 110002
info@double9books.com
www.double9books.com
Tel. 011-40042856

ABOUT THE AUTHOR

M. Jackson-Wrigley is a distinguished author renowned for his groundbreaking work, "The Film: Its Use in Popular Education." This seminal masterpiece explores the multifaceted role of cinema as a tool for education and social enlightenment. With keen insight and scholarly rigor, Jackson-Wrigley delves into the transformative power of film in shaping public consciousness and disseminating knowledge. In "The Film," Jackson-Wrigley meticulously examines how the medium of cinema transcends mere entertainment, serving as a potent vehicle for education across diverse demographics. From documentaries that shed light on pressing social issues to historical dramas that bring the past to life, he illustrates the vast educational potential inherent in cinematic storytelling. Through meticulous research and compelling analysis, Jackson-Wrigley underscores the importance of harnessing the visual language of film to engage and educate audiences in ways that traditional educational methods cannot. By exploring the use of film in classrooms, museums, and community settings, he demonstrates how this dynamic medium can foster critical thinking, empathy, and cultural awareness. "The Film: Its Use in Popular Education" stands as a testament to Jackson-Wrigley's scholarly expertise and passion for advancing education through innovative means. As a pioneering work in the field of film studies and education, it continues to inspire educators, filmmakers, and students alike, offering invaluable insights into the profound impact of cinema on society and culture.

CONTENTS

FOREWORD

I have read Mr. Jackson Wrigley's little book and I think it an admirable statement of the uses of the Film in Popular Education. It is clearly and succinctly written and its arguments are undeniable. I have just come from California where I spent nearly a year in writing films and studying the industry and art, and Mr. Wrigley is right in saying that 6,000 schools in America have cinema rooms. Quite apart from the entertainment in stories presented on the screen, there is immense value in the teaching of the film in geography, science, and natural history and topical events; and I would, if I could, put a film in every school, or rather, have films shown in every school in the land. I believe some fears have been expressed that the films may injure the eye-sight. Well, there is steady improvement in the lighting of the films, and expert medical authorities must decide as to that. Of one thing I am sure, that if injury does ensue it will be dealt with by scientific experts, and the danger will ultimately be removed.

Mr. Wrigley's book is an excellent contribution to general knowledge on the subject, and it should be widely read. The time will come, I believe, when Municipalities in England will do as is done in Wellesley, Massachusetts, and give "Municipal Movies" two days a week. I have faith that the enquiries and reports of the Cinema Commission will induce the London County Council to include the film in the educational life of the country, and that all Councils throughout the country will do the same.

Gilbert Parker.

AUTHOR'S PREFACE

Some of the matter contained in the following pages has been included in papers and lectures, and after frequent requests from various sources, I have decided to submit the whole in book form.

The topics touch upon the various phases of the value and utility of the "film" as an indispensable ally of the education and library authorities, capable of being used in the interests of both.

Other subjects of vital interest have been included, all coming within the scope of the projector. The film as an educational agency is now recognized, and the following chapters will be read, it is hoped, with interest.

M. J. W.

INTRODUCTION

The Cinema-Educator

The educational possibilities of the film have not yet been fully visualized, and this volume is designed to advance its usefulness in the widest sense in the scheme of education.

"Do not train boys to learning by force and harshness, but direct them to it by what amuses their minds," said Plato, and this in a measure is the theme of a section of this book dealing specifically with the use of the cinematograph in our schools and colleges. One can imagine the introduction of the film in class-work eliminating that Shakespearean type of scholar who goeth "like snail, unwillingly to school."

Emerson wrote to the effect that "the secret of education lies in respecting the pupil." Although he was not making allusion to the pupil of the eye, it may be that to-day "the secret of education lies in *attracting* the pupil," and the film is the important factor to secure his or her attention.

At a scholastic conference on "New Ideals in Education," at Bedford College, Miss E. Holmes affirmed that the average teacher of to-day could think of no other way of teaching than by grouping pupils into classes and educating them by chalk and talk. That meant that the older children had to mark time during the most critical years of their life, making them tired of routine, and all desire to continue education died of sheer inanition. The average teacher into whose soul had entered the iron evil of tradition could rid himself of much routine, to the advantage of himself and his pupils. Given a sympathetic Government and a sympathetic local authority, teachers might do much as they pleased in the way of striking out new paths for themselves, it is averred. The aid of the film may be one of the "new paths" to knowledge.

It has been said elsewhere that when you introduce into our schools a spirit of emulation, you have present the keenest spur admissible to the youthful intellect. The screen can convey the proper spirit to the boy and girl, whether the subject be scientific, literary, historical, or biographical. Rousseau wrote that "Education is either from nature, from man, or from things"—and the film is the modern medium. If it be truly said that the eye is the window of the soul then the possibilities of the cinematograph in our schools are without limit.

While the film can never supersede oral education, it may be most valuable as an aid to instruction. Modern educationists would not contemplate the idea of training the eye to the exclusion of the use of the ear. The cinematograph may (to use a stereotyped phrase) "supply a long-felt want."

The children of to-day are such habitual Cinema-goers that too much cinematograph is to be discouraged, but the film used in proper perspective in the schools will excite and increase interest in science, industry, art, geography, travel, history, biography and literature.

"The eye sees what it brings the power to see," said Carlyle, and the inference is obvious.

A student of child psychology (blessed word) opines that a child criminal is often the outcome of the cinema—forgetting, probably, that child-criminals existed long before the "movies" were even thought of, and overlooking the fact that "penny dreadfuls" used to be credited or discredited with this in the days gone by.

Nevertheless, the film as a new force must be recognized. At a recent Congress on Child Welfare, held in Brussels, the importance and value of the moving picture was referred to as frequently as its dangers; and it was agreed that the problem was not how to nullify, but how to harness this new power.

For the sake of the children it was proposed that a form of moral control of films should be set up. The control, it was suggested, should be exercised by a central and special commission composed of persons nominated by the Government and chosen from members of elected bodies, from associations of artists and literary people, from societies for the protection of childhood, and also from firms having an interest in the film business, producers and importers of films. Special exhibitions for children were advocated. This important phase is treated upon at some length in this volume.

The film has, however, a wider sphere than in the confines of the juvenile—that of the adolescent and the adult, summed up in the one term of "the Public."

"Public instruction should be the first object of Government," declared Napoleon (although Buonaparte never foresaw that he would be so ignominiously filmed in divers manners for the "instruction" of posterity).

It is incredible, however, how much instruction the Public receives from the cinemas. It is, therefore, an enormous power for good or for evil.

It is well to review the position in this volume and not to shirk the issue.

All manner of indictments have been levelled against the cinemas. Writers have vied with each other in their condemnation. "The producers have prostituted a noble, useful, and marvellous art before the money god of the films," it has been publicly asserted.

Much is being done to "ban" improper films, and it would be better for the reputation of the film-world if these immoral photo-plays were "taxed" out of existence. Such films are not "towards the education of your daughters," as Shakespeare writes. The Public can be its own Censor. In the meantime educationists and social-reformers can strive to guide public opinion.

"I have hope that society may be reformed, when I see how much education may be reformed," said a German writer once; and the reform of the film will come about possibly only by the people educating the film-producers to the view that it requires something else than the "adults only" brand.

While this volume advocates "direct action" against this class of film it is not intended unduly to emphasize the seamy side of the case. It is recognized to the full that there are many splendid films being "released" daily, and many managers are rendering a public service by "featuring" only the best class of picture. These many admirable productions are to be commended, and it is for the public to encourage the producers by patronizing those houses where refinement is the rule, to the exclusion of the other brand. Cinemas are public educators.

Mr. Arthur Weigall, author of "The Influence of the Kinematograph on National Life," has at various times lamented on the dullness of screen plays, making Byron's phrase in "Lara"—"dull the film"—almost a modern one. There are some film-producers who still fail to understand the mentality of a large portion of their patrons. Some films do not appeal to the intelligence of the audience. Many patrons are wearied of seeing what passes for melodrama. It would be a happy release if there were fewer "releases" of this nature. It has been said that until producers recognize that the principles of Art must come before commercial considerations the film industry is doomed.

It is for the people to insist on the best, and only the best, being "screened," and the various "corporations" that are giving us mediocre matter will be crowded out by the far-seeing producers who realize that the Public, unlike the Law, is not "a ass."

While the film can never supplant the printed word, it has been the means of directing the attention of many people to the books available at the Public Libraries. Quite recently the Rev. T. W. Pym, in an article in the "Library Association Record," said: "People will read any book which they have seen on the films, whether it be Dickens or 'George Eliot' or any other author, whom, normally, that particular person would not think of attempting to read." The cinema is thus a direct advertising medium for the Public Libraries. This phase, and the use of the cinema as a publicity service for Public Libraries, has been definitely outlined in the book on "Library Advertising," and Mr. Wrigley considerably amplifies this in the following pages.

This volume is a résumé of what has been done in film-land, and the author advances numerous original ideas that will be read with interest and profit by educationists generally, library authorities, social-reformers, and cinema-goers collectively. It is not a technical work, but the technics of the art of film production are also dealt with. After studying this volume the reader will doubtless accept Mr. Wrigley's contention that "the film is the coming apostle of education."

Walter A. Briscoe.

I
HISTORICAL

The rise and development of the cinematograph during the last few years has been truly phenomenal.

Genesis of the Film

The history of the cinematograph dates back to the obscure ages of the year 65 b.c., at which period Lucretius, in his "De Rerum Natura," made certain pertinent remarks relative to the persistence of vision—the base upon which the whole theory of motion photography is built. According to a document in the Bodleian Library at Oxford, the cinematograph has a history as far back as a.d. 130.

The first stage from which the cinematograph evolved was an invention, simplicity itself, which readily lent itself to immediate and successful development. It emanated as a toy for children, and this has been gradually built up, stage by stage, until finally completed as at the present time. I refer to that simple toy-wheel or "cycle of life;" also to the children's booklet consisting of a series of pictures of various stages of action. The leaves were held between the first finger and thumb, the little book bent backwards, and the leaves released, one by one, as quickly as possible. The whole gave the impression of the subject being in motion; and this optical illusion was the embryo of the modern motion picture.

Before the introduction of the celluloid film, animated pictures from glass plates were exhibited; but without the pliable celluloid film it is contended that cinematography would have been impracticable.

Development

The modern cinematograph was rendered possible by the invention in 1890 of the celluloid roll film, on which serial pictures are impressed by instantaneous photography; a long sensitised film being moved across the focal plane of a camera and exposed intermittently. For an hour's exhibition 50,000 to 165,000 pictures are needed. To regulate the feed in the lantern a hole is punched in the film for each picture. These holes are extremely accurate in position, and when they wear, the feed becomes irregular, and the picture "dances" in an unpleasant manner—hence that irritating feeling which arises from seeing a well-worn film vibrating. The machines have been devised in enormous numbers under the names of bioscope, biograph, kinetscope, mutograph and cinematograph, derived chiefly from Greek and Latin words for life, movement, change, etc.

The first actual attempt recorded seems to be that of a Frenchman named Louis Du Hauron, who took out two patents in 1864. Although they covered all the essential points of the modern cinematograph, the one factor which made it a failure was the slowness of the wet collodion plates of that time as compared with the gelatino-bromide. In 1906, Mr. C. Rider Noble brought out a patent whereby the moving film could be stopped at any moment for examination. Prior to this invention, the film had to speed on to the end without interruption.

New ideas and inventions seem to add improvement daily.

Present and Future

It was predicted that the cinematograph, like the skating rink, would have a short life and die in its infancy, but this was a mistaken idea—the "movies," like "Liza," have "come to stay." They are a force to be reckoned with. It would not be overstating the fact to say that more people attend the cinema than all other places of entertainment massed together.

The returns relative to the cinema industry are immense. Regarding attendances at these places in this country, it shows no fewer than 1,075,875,000 attendances at cinema exhibitions in the course of a single year. In the British Isles there are approximately 4,500 theatres with a seating capacity of accommodating one in every thirty-seven of the population. Upon working out these figures it shows that the entire population of the United Kingdom visits cinema exhibitions on an average once a fortnight. About 5,000 new subjects are issued each year, and some 70,000,000 feet of film are running through the projectors each week. From 80,000 to 100,000 persons are directly engaged in the various branches of the trade.

Its increased popularity in the future is assured, and its progress will depend largely upon what uses the nation makes of this new force in national education.

II
EDUCATIONAL

The Cinematograph in Schools

Various boroughs have made forward steps in the introduction of the cinematograph in the school. The Birmingham Juvenile Organization Committee has prepared an exceedingly readable and interesting report for presentation to the Birmingham Education Committee. To expand upon this theory, an open exhibition is to be arranged and will be attended by thousands of children from the senior departments of the schools, the younger element being excluded. Teachers and officials of the Local Education Authority will lend their support.

A synopsis of prepared notes was given to the teachers and scholars. The schools are to be formed into groups, so that pupils may attend a special performance at a convenient centre at regular intervals. The programme of exhibition is to last for one hour; the films selected coming under five headings:—

(1) Literature,
(2) Geography,
(3) Science,
(4) Natural History,
(5) Composition.

Literature is represented by a pictorial representation of "The Merchant of Venice." It is argued that by this method the children will be induced to turn to the plays after they have seen the characters portrayed upon the screen.

One feature missing is that the film cannot give the child any idea of the beauty of Shakespeare's prose and verse. In the case of geography it is apparent that the film can efficiently take the place of the text-book. Science and natural history could be represented by films showing the life-history of the salmon and the silkworm. One suggested experiment dealing with composition is that a portion of the story be shown, and that when the children have returned to the school they should be asked to invent a title or to summarize the film as far as it has been shown, and complete it according to their own ideas. At a future sitting the remaining portion of the film would be exhibited and the children would then compare it with their own efforts.

A similar exhibition was given in Manchester before members of the Stretford Education Committee. In this instance a portable projector was used, the lighting circuit being tapped for electric power. It is openly admitted that the cinematograph has a wide field, but the idea that the cinema will ever supplant the text-book is considered unlikely.

One would like to know the definite view adopted by the Commissioners as regards educational films and the benefits derived therefrom. Many authorities are still stumbling along in the dark, unwilling to make a beginning, but they cannot maintain this attitude for long, because the forward march of the utility of the cinema in the school is becoming apparent, and all education authorities who are apostles of progress will have to toe the line.

The Film as Teacher

When it is remembered that the moving picture camera may be used in connection with the microscope, that it has an unlimited field in geography, in the recording of social life, and in natural history—it seems difficult to account for the fact that universities and colleges have passed it by. The value is not so much to be sought in the classroom, for there are, of course, objections to its use there, but the founding of this new type of library would possess an interest for future generations which can scarcely be over-estimated.

There is no doubt that the decision of the London County Council upon the question of using the film as a part of the educational curriculum, will, in the main, be governed by the nature of the Report issued by the Special Committee appointed by the National Council of Public Morals to consider the part the cinematograph is destined to play in public education.

The Education Committee was instructed to report as to the provision by the Council of the facilities on an educational basis to enable all London school children to see cinematograph films. These were placed under the following heads:—

(*a*) Purely instructional or educational; travel, science, and natural history.

(*b*) Suitable in other respects for exhibition to a juvenile audience.

Certain objections were raised. One fundamental difficulty was eyestrain, and another, ill-ventilated rooms. The whole problem is being viewed by experts from a technical, psychological, and physiological standpoint.

They had exhibited before them a film showing the power to teach history and geography. This was demonstrated in a remarkable way by an exhibition film relating to Christopher Columbus. The scenario was in Spain, for the most part in the actual surroundings associated with Columbus. There could be no better way of demonstrating to the scholar the trials and difficulties encountered by Columbus before and after he realized his life's ambition.

It was contended that it would be better to arrange a series of lectures beforehand, explaining at some length the persecution endured by Columbus. By this means an oral and visional teaching would be enacted, leaving a more lasting impression than would be attainable otherwise.

Some Educational Films

To-day Shakespeare is reeled off a spool, and human life taught at the end of a crank. You may travel over land and sea without leaving your seat and see great personages of the world perform their mighty deeds, and unconsciously knowledge of life and the world is derived which makes a difference in the conception of things surrounding us.

The average member of a community fails to comprehend the significance of the new and powerful agency in education. All this means a revolution in pedagogy, the scrapping of text-books in favour of the film. It means a vividness where before had been vagueness. It means a true visualization and realization of life, where hitherto an indefinite printed description of it was acquired. In this country gatherings of teachers have been vividly impressed by animated photography. By means of the silent teacher, young and old have learned more about the physical, industrial and social geography of the world during the past few years than during any previous quarter of a century. It brings vividly before our eyes the idea of intense cold, atmospheric conditions, blizzards, and life peculiar to the regions around the Poles; and, again, the sweltering heat, vegetation, methods of living and transport in the tropics. One is brought face to face with the primitive life, habits, and customs of the aborigines of the least known corners of the world; while even life immediately around us is revealed in a manner which hitherto has been impossible.

Take a film about the volcano, of which most children have heard but never seen. It would explain that a volcano throws up smoke, calcined dust, red-hot stones, and melted matter called lava. The summit is hollowed out in a great excavation having the shape of a funnel, sometimes miles in circumference. The principal volcanoes could be shown, as Vesuvius, near Naples; Etna, in Sicily; Hecla, in Iceland.

A curtain of smoke filling the orifice of the crater denotes the forthcoming eruption. When the air is calm the smoke rises vertically to nearly a mile in height, finally spreading out like a huge blanket, cutting off the rays of the sun, and sinking down on the volcano, covering it with a dense smoke-cloud. A huge sheaf of fire bursts from the crater to a height of 6,000 ft., and the heavy cloud is illuminated by the fiery red of the sky. Millions of sparks dart out like vivid lightning to the summit of the blazing sheaf. These sparks, so small from a distance, are, in reality, incandescent masses of stone, and of a sufficient momentum to crush the most solid structure in their fall.

From the bowels of the mountain through the volcanic chimney ascends a flux of melted mineral substance, or lava, pouring out into the crater, forming a lake of dazzling fire in the sun. Through the crevasses as well as over the edges of the crater the lava flows in streams. The fiery current, formed of dazzling and paste-like matter, similar to melted metal, advances slowly; the front of the lava stream represents a rampart on fire. Animals and human beings flee before it, but all objects stationary are lost. Trees are seen to blaze a moment on contact with the lava and sink down reduced to charcoal; the thickest walls impeding its progress are calcined and collapse; the hardest rocks are vitrified, melted. The flow of lava eventually subsides; the subterranean vapours, forced by the enormous pressure of the solid mass, escape with greater violence than ever, carrying with them whirlwinds of fine dust floating in sinister clouds and sinking down upon the neighbouring plain. Finally the mountain ceases its activity and peace reigns again for an indefinite time.

Visualize the terrible eruption of Mt. Etna in Sicily of two hundred years ago. A dark night preceded the storm. Trees swayed like reeds buffeted by the wind; people fled to avoid being crushed under the ruins of their dwellings. They lost their footing on the quaking ground and fell. Mt. Etna burst into a fissure ten miles long, and along this fissure broke forth a number of volcanic mouths, vomiting clouds of black smoke and calcined sand. Soon seven of these mouths were united in one abyss emitting cinders and lava.

Torrents of lava poured from all the crevasses of the mountain down upon the plain, destroying houses, forests and crops. The stream reached the walls of Catania and spread over the country. There, as if to demonstrate its strength to the terrified Catanians, it tore away a hill and transplanted it some distance; it lifted in one mass a field planted with vines and let it float for some time, until the green was reduced to charcoal and disappeared.

A fierce battle ensued between lava and water. The lava presented a perpendicular front nearly a mile in length and forty feet high. At the touch of that burning wall, which continued plunging further and further into the waves, enormous masses of vapour rose with terrible hissings, darkened the sky with their thick clouds, and fell in a salt rain over the region. In a few days the lava had made the limits of the shore recede three hundred and fifty yards.

The stream, swollen with new tributaries, grew from day to day and approached the town. The inhabitants could be seen from the top of the walls watching the implacable scourge. The lava finally reached the ramparts. The fiery flood rose slowly but it rose ceaselessly. It finally touched the top of the walls, whereupon, yielding to pressure, they were overthrown for the length of forty-five yards, and the stream of fire penetrated the town.

The last scene was that of the inhabitants fleeing in terror. What a realistic geography lesson, never to be forgotten, would a film of this description make!

The films can show anything from the mining of coal to the manufacture of the needle; from the weaving of a dainty handkerchief to the building of a battleship. The films projected would be purely educational, though there are numerous incidents shown, which amuse and entertain, in addition to imparting information. A particular film series of an educational and scientific nature is now available.

The Smith-Urban "Kinemacolour" series depicting the budding flowers and the opening of blossoms—which in nature occupies several days—are disclosed with uncanny realism in less than two minutes.

Marvels of the universe, a scientific film of nature-study and general knowledge, finds many patrons.

History Taught by Film

It would be necessary for historians to collaborate very closely with the producers in the preparation of historical films. The mere fact of being called upon to provide a scene for a picture and a detailed explanation, however, would go far to arouse a new enthusiasm in their work among students and teachers of history. It might assist us to vision our forefathers out of their portrait frames and parish churches, which are, perhaps, their only extant monuments, and reveal them to us as they lived and moved.

In most cases the educative value was confined to actual performers, or those who took part in the preparation of costumes, and in general the action of a scene was too far removed from the audience for close observation and too quickly over for effective study.

Supposing one could produce a film, actually showing the scenes enacted during the life and times of the Romans; depicting their daily life, court ceremonial and ancient coronations, or their judicial proceedings, their tournaments,—we should add materially to our historical knowledge of the people; and one must not lose sight of the fact, that when we have passed to the "Great Beyond," and the world still continues to be inhabited some thousands of years hence, populated with people actuated with the same ideas, the same aspirations as ourselves, our present period will stand exactly in a similar relationship,—in regard to time at least.

What could present a more magnificent visual panorama than the procession of events of the Elizabethan period to the eighteenth century, laying open to our view their lives, the arts and crafts of their time, and our progress is then made over the stepping-stones of the past? Imagine the royal events of history, the gorgeous scenes of the coronations of English kings, as they succeeded each other.

Supposing an authoritative film could have been produced of the Great War, showing the whole of Europe in conflict, from the invasion of Belgium to the Armistice. The whole of the incidents—the devastation of property by the mighty engines of war; refugees in flight from the oncoming enemy; the heroic attacks and defence by the British soldiers in spite of tremendous odds; the want, misery and suffering following in the train.

The scope of the cinematograph for educational purposes could be considerably widened by children and adults being shown how things have been and are being done. The use of colour films for explaining history would enable the teacher to demonstrate the growth of British Dominion in India—for instance, Bombay could be represented by a tiny red speck, which would expand in correct historical sequence until the whole of the peninsula was covered. The development of the colouring, as this or that successful campaign was completed, would explain to observers, more explicitly than any printed list, the political effects of history. The scenes would thus be indelibly impressed upon the minds of children. And the same idea might be extended to the other colonies, Canada, Australia, New Zealand, South Africa, etc., depicting their history from the first settlement to the complete establishment of the Overseas dominions and their activities of to-day. The film, in short, is a fine medium for political propaganda if wisely used.

The following subjects lend themselves to effective treatment as film productions for educational purposes: the growth of the European Colonies, the rise and fall of the Ottoman Empire, the decline and renaissance of Poland, the historical groupings of the various States of Europe in the wars of the eighteenth and nineteenth centuries, to name but a few.

The Film in American Schools

The use of films in American schools is already an accomplished fact and is generally recognised as a great educational asset.

The American Red Cross during the War found it extremely useful in aiding its work, and it was decided, in view of the coming of peace, to extend this work and build it upon a solid and permanent base. A Bureau of Pictures was established and an important branch was the origin of a sister Bureau for Europe, its headquarters being in Paris; the aim in view being the formation of a library of films, demonstrating to the New World how the Old World lived and how it had suffered during the War.

The incentive for the development of this idea by the Red Cross was created by urgent representations made by thousands of schools and churches throughout the length and breadth of the United States, a stirring appeal which could not be ignored.

A popular feature in the early days of the educational curriculum was the extensive use of the magic-lantern hour, in which inanimate pictures were thrown upon a screen. This was capital as far as it went, but obviously the cinema could be utilised with a far greater effect and satisfaction. From the commercial standpoint it was found that the monetary return from the exhibition of "educational films" was not satisfactory. One film featuring Mary Pickford would produce greater profits than a perfect and complete library of educational films!

The churches wishing to give film entertainments on Sunday found the ordinary films not suitable to their needs and sought outside aid. The American Red Cross bridged the gap. Thousands of schools and churches are now in touch with this Picture Bureau, whose work is administered through fourteen divisions by which this movement is governed, and every independent division is building up its own library of specially selected films. The aim and object is to procure films of educational, scenic, hygienic, and industrial interest. It also endeavours to cement the allied friendship and cordial international relations between the two great Anglo-Saxon peoples.

This Bureau is equipped with a large and efficient staff of expert photographers, and when a film is taken this is duplicated and a copy is dispatched to every division, accompanied by a list of subjects which are at the service of the schools, and if a certain demand is shown for special films, this demand is supplied.

The range of subjects when this project has matured will be illimitable, and it will be possible to co-ordinate them so that they can be absorbed into the recognised curriculum. It has been proved that children are interested even by isolated subjects, contradicting any contention that a child does not remember a lesson which it receives by means of the "movies." This film lesson provides a welcome break in the text-book grind, and is the most popular and eagerly sought feature in the school.

From an international aspect, the value of the film is undoubted. All the American children will by this means be able to visualize the marvels of Europe, and, in addition, form an idea of the surroundings in which many of their fathers and brothers made the supreme sacrifice in the defence of humanity.

These Red Cross films seen in their schools will convey to them exactly what is being done, and in this way the film will take its place as an ambassador of perfect understanding, cementing the already friendly relations existing between the two countries. Over 6,000 schools in America have cinema rooms and practically every new school being erected in America is equipped with an up-to-date cinema-operating room and theatre.

It behoves England to make greater strides if she is to keep abreast of the times. The question is asked: "What are we waiting for before taking the plunge into this educative speculation?" Possibly the deterrent is the belated appearance of the completed inquiries of the "Cinema Commission." If it is truthfully said that England is ten years behind the American in dentistry, the same period applies as regards the possibilities of the cinema in relation to the school.

A conference of well-known educationists recently assembled at Columbia University, U.S.A., to examine a number of film subjects on geography, biology, industry, and popular astronomy, collected for the purpose by the National Committee for Better Films. The affiliated Committee for Better Films has asked for suggestions and criticisms regarding safety precautions, methods of furnishing pictures in large quantities and other matters.

The Federation of Child Study in conjunction with the Women's City Club, the National Committee for Better Films and the Juvenile Motion

Picture League, have formulated a scheme by which entertainments suitable for young people are given in the various picture theatres on Fridays and Saturdays, for which the Committee select the films to be shown and guarantee an audience. The University of the State of New York are making every endeavour to promote "visual education." The town of Wellesley, Massachusetts, has "municipal movies" two days a week. The State censorship is strongly opposed on the ground that what is required is selection and not censorship.

Instructing the Deaf Mute

"List with thine eyes, and I will list with mine," is a revised version of a well-known quotation which applies with considerable point to the modern mode of conversation between deaf mutes, who are taught, by the close observation of the movements of a speaker's lips, to see, instead of to hear, what is being said. This is where the cinema may help our less fortunate brothers and sisters. An effective film could be prepared which would depict with great precision the lip action which takes place as the various letters of the alphabet are being articulated, and also the similar change of appearance visible, as groups of letters or words are uttered. Such an alphabet and the graphic record of speech, available for use over and over again, enabling mute pupils to commit to heart, would make a tedious task simplified.

In Mental Hospitals

The effect of the film upon the healthy mind is obvious, and its introduction in various mental hospitals is now in the experimental stage. Cinematograph entertainment has already been provided in one of the Birmingham mental asylums, and it is anticipated that the exhibitions will materially help in the recovery of the patients.

Medical Students

The "daily press" tells us that the medical profession is the latest convert to the cinematograph as an aid to instruction. The instrument is being utilized to record operations, for presentation before medical students, and in this manner a large number of unnecessary operations will be prevented. It is maintained that many intricate and delicate operations can be more lucidly expounded to the student by these biographic demonstrations than is possible in the operating theatre, during the carrying out of an operation, or by means of anatomic diagrams.

Processes of bone-grafting have been thrown upon the screen. Serial radiographs of the stomach showing all the stages of digestion have been revealed to an audience of surgeons. One professor of neurology uses twenty-five thousand feet of cinema film in teaching and illustrating nervous and mental diseases. Even the blood has not escaped the cinema-worker's relentless probing. By means of the ultra-micro-cinematograph the corpuscles of the blood are magnified to an enormous degree and one is able to follow with ease precisely what happens when the vital fluid is contaminated by different foreign organisms, and the terrific struggle that ensues for supremacy, and the exact action produced by the administration of various curative specifics. It is evident that, in the battle against human disease and death, the moving picture is destined to play an astonishing part.

The Great War has provided some interesting surgical opportunities, which, had they been witnessed by those other than medical students, would have been gruesome and revolting, yet are interesting to the strong-nerved who can withstand the odour of the warm blood of human life. Take the case of a soldier shot in the thigh by machine-gun bullets which have made the head of the femur resemble a sand sieve; watch the film, from the carrying of the patient from the ward to the theatre, the administration of the anæsthetic, and the deep-chested breathing of the patient who gradually succumbs to the sweet pungent odour; note the interested audience of white-robed sisters, nurses and surgeons; the well-placed incision, the parting of the sinews and muscles, and the removal of the head of the "femur" to be replaced later by an exact replica in silver.

In medical science the cinematograph should become a most important aid in the instruction of students.

III
LIBRARIES AND LITERATURE

School, Library, and Cinema

What a force to be reckoned with would be the combined efforts of school, library and cinema as factors in education. These two former sections have become more united during the last few years. It is only recently that the activities of the Public Library Authorities have been fully appreciated by the Education Authorities. The outlook is now brighter, and a recognized harmony exists; their efforts now being united for the furtherance of educational ideals.

All educational aims should be to broaden, deepen, improve and strengthen the childish imagination, both sympathetic and intellectual. If used without proper supervision, there is not a more harmful agency than the cinema.

Mention is made elsewhere of the Cinema Commission, the London County Council, and the Birmingham Education Committee and what they are undertaking on behalf of the school.

Film Collections

A nucleus could be a collection of twenty films; four dealing with classics; four with the surrounding things of everyday life, forming general knowledge; four dealing with foreign countries, their social life, games, customs, etc.; four dealing with entomology, zoology, etc.; four depicting the commercial life, showing shipbuilding yards, steel works, cotton and woollen factories, pottery manufacture, etc. These films would broaden the views and strengthen the imagination of children.

The nucleus thus being formed, the films could be circulated throughout the surrounding counties, boroughs and towns; being exhibited at the local library once a week. In conjunction with these films, "reading lists" could be prepared of books for home-reading, and widely distributed. A change of film could be made once a week, which means that before the stock of films had completed one round, five months would elapse, giving ample time in which to procure future additions.

By bringing the cinema within his scope of activities, the librarian adds materially to the usefulness of the library to the community at large, proving the sterling worth of such an institution to the town. How this financial venture is to be met and supported will be the inevitable question, the answer to which is by co-operation; each town or borough taking a share of the burden and contributing financially towards their maintenance. An endeavour must be made to get the local Education Authority interested, and the battle is partly won. Submit to them a practical scheme, on a sound business footing, attractive and definite, and they will, after careful consideration, give unstintingly their financial support.

The whole of the country could be divided into areas, such as North-Eastern, North-Western, South-Eastern, South-Western, etc., where towns, etc., like Stretford, Manchester, Stockport, Bolton, Wigan, Liverpool, Southport and Chester could all produce a repertoire of film subjects. Each Authority could be responsible for the production of films relative to their own manufacture, which could be mapped out as follows:—

(1) Denton and Stockport, for hat manufacture, showing the whole of the process felt goes through, from the raw material to the finished "Sandringham."

(2) Bradford could give a tour of the woollen mills.

(3) Nottingham the lace trade.

(4) Hanley the pottery trade.

(5) Oldham and Leigh the cotton trade.

(6) Atherton, etc., coal mining.

(7) Liverpool, the docks and shipping.

(8) Kent, for the strawberry and hop-growing industries.

(9) Devonport, the dockyards, etc., etc.

There is ample scope for the treatment of such subjects.

As described elsewhere, a Central Bureau could be established, every film classified according to subject, and from this Bureau would emanate a steady flow of purely educational films—teaching or imparting knowledge in a popular manner.

Again, where space does not permit, either in the schools or the local library, the allied sympathy of the managers of the local cinemas could be obtained, and one film could be inserted as part of their programme, securing for them the necessary audience, and at the same time advertising the Education Authority and the Library.

The aim of all libraries is to preserve knowledge for succeeding generations, and films such as those described in the preceding chapter—that portion dealing with history taught by the film—would be of permanent value for reference.

The general idea of providing a permanent record of historical events in the nation's history is worthy of universal encouragement, and also of making these records easily accessible for public enlightenment.

It has been said that the public library should reflect every phase of mental activity, not only the high and educational kind, but also of the recreative, the social side of life. A vast amount of enlightenment and instruction, with remarkable force and rapidity, can be conveyed by the aid of the cinematograph. "Every picture tells a story," whether it be of wonder or beauty, or of travels and national customs; some enlightenment may be gained from the exhibition. The seed sown by the pictures of this or that city, whether abroad or at home, may, eventually, be reaped in improved conditions of life and its surroundings. A clearer conception, a more sensible interpretation of the wonderful things around us, is shown than could ever be conveyed by a professor's treatise, or an artist's impressions.

Preservation of the Film

Libraries in general have failed to appreciate the educational value of the cinematograph during the growth of the last fifteen years. For years now the National Board of Censorship has been urging the development of the use of educational films.

The first attempt at anything in the nature of a Lending Library of Films was inaugurated by Gaumont & Co., in 1904. The scheme enabled the amateur or professional possessor of a cinematograph-projecting apparatus, to hire or loan on reasonable terms a selection of film subjects, so that by the outlay of one guinea per night, the private exhibitor could command an inexhaustible supply of film subjects.

There are a number of elements entering into the production, distribution, and the public exhibition of pictures. The raw stock of celluloid from which films are manufactured has a limited existence. The base of the film is usually of a highly inflammable composition. Again, before the pictures are perfected, for public exhibition, the producer's outfit should include highly perfected cameras, studios, staging, and star actors, and a search, often, for appropriate outdoor settings for the scenes to be enacted. The skilful direction of people and scenes to obtain illusions requires an expert at the business; for it necessitates a high grade of technical ability for the production of scenic, travel, and scientific pictures with the minimum film waste. Once the picture has been constructed, prepared with subjects and sub-titles, and has been submitted to the Board of Censorship, it must be extensively advertised, circulated amongst exchanges throughout the kingdom, and the commands of the public exhibitors awaited. All these complicated processes have emanated from the regular daily demand of the people for entertainment, not necessarily enlightenment. The manufacturers know the percentage of film subjects demanded, whether tragic, thrilling, artistic, humorous, or educational.

I will give some idea as to the film. Each picture in size is roughly three-quarters by one inch; the average length of a black and white film is 1000 feet, giving a total of 16,000 pictures. When rolled this film fills a tin box—allowing for the fact that it is round—equal to the size of a royal octavo volume, but considerably heavier. Thus it is evident that the question of space is unimportant. The number of films produced and published does not equal the number of books published in the same time. A great number of the films published are unsuitable for preservation, and, therefore, would find no place in a National Historical Repository.

The method of the present classification of books would be applied to the classification of the films, covering, as they do, historical, scientific, artistic, and technical subjects. The life of the film depends upon its treatment. The period varies, but when in daily use it should last for twelve years; and, if every care has been taken, and the film is seldom used, it will last for fifty years. Twenty-five years may be taken as a fair average under ordinary methods. Of course, new films can be reprinted from the old, and therefore, no film need be discarded.

A fairly satisfactory solution of the difficulty of making provision for a regular service of films at a minimum cost would be the appropriation, annually, by the State, of a sufficient sum to allow the purchase of a number of the best films by State Libraries, or (seeing that libraries now come under the protecting wing of the Education Authorities) by a State Department of Education. This increasing library of films could be held at the disposal of Library Authorities who contribute towards its acquisition and maintenance.

Library of Films in Berlin

In October, 1914, a "Library of Films" was opened in Berlin. This Berlin depository already possesses a very large collection of valuable films, dealing especially with scientific and allied subjects, which is probably unequalled elsewhere. In connection with the library an Intelligence Bureau has been opened, where advice can be obtained on all matters connected with the cinematograph and its uses.

Its resources are inexhaustible and the films may be borrowed for purposes of instruction by Educational Authorities and other allied bodies. It is established for the national preservation of historical and other films, and will become invaluable as the years roll on, from the historic point of view.

Advertising the Library

I was once asked the question, "Why do not libraries give greater publicity to their activities, means and resources, and not be satisfied with the fact that they are merely performing an everyday public function, expected of them as a municipal institution which gives some sort of return to the ratepayers for the rate levied upon them for its maintenance?"

True, some of the ratepayers are quite satisfied when they can go to the local library and borrow one or two books to while away a few leisure hours during a wet week-end. Herein lies a small conception of what a public library is for.

The library at the present time, if it is to maintain its popularity, must be aggressive and not passive. We must not be content to rest on our oars and survey what we have done with a complacent smile of satisfaction, and say, "I have done my best," but we must think what we can do next to keep the vision of usefulness of the public library ever before the public. The library is like the tree in nature, once it ceases to grow it commences to decay, and this food for further thought must be provided by the initiative of the librarian, providing he is an enthusiast. If cheap stories so often depicted could be replaced by such films as "The Odyssey," "Hamlet," "Evangeline," the cinematograph would become a distinct influence for good.

It has been voiced at some of the conferences that systematized propaganda work is needed. I am glad to see that the Library Association has at last awakened to the fact that the educational value of the Public Library is not known as it should be. The appointment of a "Publicity Committee" shows that a determined effort is being made to launch out into something original, and, I hope, something which will demand world-wide attention.

Anyone interested in Library work cannot fail to see that such a popular and powerful agent as the film must have an effect upon the Public Libraries. Cinemas are not on the wane, but are considerably on the increase. Now that the ban on "luxury building" has been removed, these buildings—in some cases "super-cinemas" embodying every convenience—will spring up everywhere. One very seldom, if ever, hears of a cinema being "wound up for bankruptcy; these picture-houses are too popular, and this popularit will remain as long as one generation succeeds another.

The film can arouse an enthusiasm in heretofore disinterested readers and expose to them the pleasures and joys of life they are missing, and onl the totally illiterate can ignore it.

Possibly it is not generally known by librarians that managers o cinemas are genial individuals, willing to oblige in a little library publicity and where the library is in close proximity, so much the better.

What I refer to is a "screened advertisement" on behalf of the librar authorities, calling attention to the fact that the book from which the filn is produced may be borrowed from the Central Library and its branches which medium has been advocated in Mr. Walter Briscoe's book on "Librar Advertising."

Here is the idea for a permanent local "publicity" campaign, and in du course the Library Association, backed up by Government recognition, ma launch out into a national programme of recognition.

Some may advocate publicity by means of specially trained orators who would demonstrate from public platforms in forcible arguments th advantages of the Public library; others may convene dinner-hour meeting and deliver speeches to working men and women as during an election others may urge the use of public hoardings or electric signs in publi places, changing colour every few seconds.

It is admitted that the Press is a powerful organ, proclaiming to ever reading individual items of interest within its pages. This is good so far as i goes. Possibly advertising in it would be repaid where the paper has acces to every home, and even then there is the possibility of its being overlooked unless the headline be emblazoned in red. Some people when perusing thei favourite papers look for one thing of interest to them only. Some scan th stock and share markets; others devour the racing news; some look at th advertisement columns in the hope of finding a house to let; the gentler se invariably peruse the bargain sales—so there is a danger of library matter being overlooked.

Some new tactics must be tried; something which will yield bette results, something which will meet the gaze of young or old—and ther is that all-powerful national appealing projector, the cinematograph. Thi will explain with greater efficiency than either the public Press, the hoarse voiced orator, or any other medium.

People who remain ignorant or illiterate need no longer remain in this stage. If they do not know the alphabet, they can be taught it; if they cannot write they can be shown how to wield a pen, and the various styles of writing—backhand, roundhand, copper-plate or script, all by means of text-books obtainable at the library.

The poorest man, without any visible means, living in a garret, has this store of wealth at his disposal just for the asking. Anyone wishing to become acquainted with a foreign language to aid him in his business can learn by the "self-taught series." Thousands of people in these circumstances could be made acquainted with the treasures of the library by means of the film.

"Publicity Films"

The Public Library "Lending Department" would make an admirable film, showing, as it would, borrowers selecting their books and being assisted by the library assistants. Continuing, the books themselves could be shown in the process of opening. In the natural history section the various phases of nature would be seen by the eye; the philology section would disclose the people of the various ages, dressed in keeping with the period, and the language they spoke; and the literary section would open to view the poets of the various ages and the poems they wrote.

A book-stack would revolve; a book would open in the historical section on the history of England, showing early Britons in their prehistoric dress, and these would change as the various periods in the nation's history was passed through.

Here is the chance of a lifetime for the exponents of the uses and utility of the Library of which they should take every advantage. There are some people who do not even know that public libraries actually exist in their midst, and what facilities they freely offer. They have yet to realize that the Library is in reality the People's University, instituted to enable everyone to acquire knowledge and enlightenment.

It would not be impossible to prepare a film on a much wider scale, the production of which would probably run into similar figures to those of the biggest "releases." (I hope readers will not blame me for being an idealist!) For national publicity purposes a film on "The Public Library: its Evolution and Possibilities" could be prepared, depicting the remarkable modern growth of this valuable institution. The veil of obscurity could be torn aside, and that erroneous impression dispelled that the library is a very modern institution. The interested person could retrace his steps in the annals of library history as far back as it is possible to go.

Library History

Before our eyes would actually be shown the fact that books themselves were not always of the material so familiar to us. Knowledge could be extended far beyond the invention of the printing-press; metal, stone, bricks, walls, pillars, and even the rocks of Nature's own production were used to convey information to succeeding generations. We should be brought into close contact with the libraries of Assyria, Babylonia and Chaldea, the three ancient empires of which the most is known. There will be seen the palace-temple of Nippur, founded not later than 2280 b.c., the "tomes" classified and catalogued on shelves in the most approved manner, some 200,000 clay bricks being exhibited.

The period of the Greeks would prove interesting, storing the archives in the temples of the Gods, during the sixth century b.c. The Romans would be pictured amassing their libraries as spoils of war; the first to be established in 168 b.c. by Aemilius Paulus—the librarian being a slave or freeman. Time progresses with the passing of the film—Bishop Alexander is seen establishing the first Christian library at Jerusalem in a.d. 212. The libraries later meet with a catastrophe, being swept away by the invasion of the Goths and barbarians of the Western Empire in the fifth century. From the fall of the Western Empire to the Revival of Learning in the fifteenth century the libraries passed into the hands of the monks, who were the collectors of the Middle Ages. Here they could appear, working in the monasteries, writing on parchment rolls. Every Benedictine house was equipped with a library.

Interest quickens as the rapid growth of libraries in England becomes apparent—at Jarrow, Lichfield, Whitby, and other places in the North of England. The gradual developments from these libraries to early town libraries, the various types, remodelled to suit the requirements demanded by mental enlightenment, would all create interest and pleasure.

The modern library would prove the most interesting. The shelves upon shelves of books, closely classified, yet so simple, would evoke admiration. The visual procession of saints and sages, warriors and martyrs, the upholders of justice and freedom, as they stepped from their places upon the shelves, would create wonderment.

Single shelves bridge the intervals of time; generations upon generations of men congregate there.

From the film, the demonstration shows that through the medium of books one can witness the plague of Athens or London, without contagion;

follow Caesar upon his marches; stand by the side of Agricola as he regards Ireland and says that some day he will "go over and take it"; rove the Dark Continent with Stanley, and learn the secrets of artificial and natural flight with Sir Hiram Maxim. Similarly, readers would transport their thoughts according to the nature of the literature indulged in by them.

It could be shown that no matter what our tastes are, whether they be inventive or whether we prefer to be in the company of a celebrated humourist, the library will supply all wants.

Other activities in connection with the Library could be shown: the travelling libraries setting out to the rural districts, the door-to-door calls, the issuing of books to our isolated brethren. Lastly, our work with the children in the juvenile library and reading rooms, and the establishment of libraries in the schools.

What more material can the publicity exponent desire than lies here within his reach—the film for perfect propaganda work? It only needs to be utilized. By means of one human effort for the creation of such a film, its duplication to any number, its use either in the libraries, the local cinema, or public hall, the whole of the population of England could be enlightened simultaneously or gradually, and the efforts of the publicists would be rewarded by the Public Library being placed in its right sphere as an educational institution; its use to the community would be recognized and the demand upon its resources would be increased.

We as librarians, custodians of books, must acknowledge the significance of the cinematograph. We have in projectors a valuable aid to our works as educators. The "movies" are the coming apostles of education; in them we have the world in miniature, and its value as an educative force can hardly be over-estimated. In a very few years every well-equipped library will be installed with its own cinematograph apparatus, and possibly its own asbestos-lined cinema-operating room, as at Stockport, for instance.

The Book.

A film on the making of a book could be made decidedly interesting, showing the many processes that go to the making of a book; from the arrival of the manuscript to the purchase of the book at a shop, and the customer reading it at home. Such a film has been prepared by Messrs. Doubleday Page & Co., Garden City, New York. The film can portray the living characters of books, and readers usually derive more pleasure from reading after the characters have been portrayed upon the screen.

The Film as Mental Ally

Much enlightenment may be derived from the film. There are some people, who during their lifetime spend too much time on petty details, a fair proportion of every community are totally incapable of following any line of thought to its logical conclusion. Some people, whilst reading a book, have to depend upon a bookmark to locate the place where they are reading, instead of being able to pick up the book and recommence, remembering where they discontinued previously. Concentration of thought whilst reading, a complete assimilation of the facts contained in the book, and the capability of understanding what has been read, would obviate the necessity of any temporary bookmark. The fact of remembering what has been read will readily indicate the place to recommence reading.

Some people will read a novel, and at the end cannot recall the characters in the book, or what part they have taken in the story. Such a hapless habit is to be deprecated. Others possess a more retentive memory and read a book with a definite purpose, and at the conclusion, or even some considerable time afterwards, could enumerate every detail, fit in every character, the moral they present, and even tell one the defects therein. To such people as the forementioned, the film would be of great assistance; not only to give a correct rendering, visually, of the book, but to help them to remember facts and characters.

There are the class of people, few in number, who own and use their own libraries, and have little use for the Public Library. Another class, slightly larger, but still, numerically, only a small portion of the population, know books and use the Public Library freely and with intelligence. The remainder, or more than half the average community, need to be taught its value and purpose.

Filmed Literature

The "movies" make their appeal through the rapidity with which the plot of the story is carried along, and the exaggerated emphasis with which the different points are brought out. It is a primary or kindergarten for the schooling of those people into the region of emotional experiences. By co-operating with the "movies" the Library in time might be able to grade the work so that a brief and simple love-story might be heard or read with understanding. The repetition of the visual presentation of the idea possible in a moving picture would help to make its meaning clear.

Take a novel as an example: in this case Ethel M. Dell's "The Keeper of the Door." The chief character is the doctor or surgeon, who makes every endeavour to retain life in the human body, he being the keeper of the door, not allowing the spirit to depart. There is something really beautiful as this picture is portrayed: the vigilance of the doctor, and the kindness and patience of the nurse; yet in spite of all this attention the activity of the patient is slowly waning, and then the last breath is taken and human life ceases to be.

Other features create interest—the surroundings, the way the characters play their part, and the emblematical representations all create a longing to read the book. In reading, the whole scenes return as witnessed; greater interest is created, and one cannot imagine a person losing his place of reading, or the inability to fit the characters in their places, even after some considerable time has elapsed.

IV
SOCIAL

The Cinema Commission

The National Council of Public Morals embraces many subjects in its activities; for some years it has been keenly interested in the influence of the cinematograph upon young people, with the possibilities of its development and with its adaptation to national educational purposes. The President (the Bishop of Birmingham), with the Rev. F. B. Meyer, D.D., took a leading part; the first Cinematograph Congress being held at Olympia in 1913.

The Commission did not seek to abuse the people responsible for the promotion of the cinema by outspoken raillery, but met representatives of the whole trade in frank discussion of the best means of ridding the community of whatever evil elements existed, and meeting the demands of the best public opinion for a higher class programme; suitable exhibitions for juvenile minds, for the suppression of certain evils which had temporarily blighted the cinema halls, and lastly for the establishment of a national censorship which would give the necessary freedom for the proper development of the cinematograph, whilst prohibiting all undesirable films.

At a meeting held in London on November 24, 1916, representatives of the Cinematograph Trade Council, the Incorporated Association of Kinematograph Manufacturers, Ltd., the Kinematograph Renters' Society of Great Britain and Ireland met together, and it was finally resolved—

> "That the National Council of Public Morals be requested to institute an independent inquiry into the physical, social, moral, and educational influence of the cinema, with special reference to young people."

The terms of reference to the Commission were:—

> (1) To institute an inquiry into the physical, social, educational, and moral influences of the cinema, with special reference to young people.
>
> (2) The present position and future development of the cinematograph, with special reference to social and educational value and possibilities.

(3) To investigate the nature and extent of the complaints which have been made against the cinematograph exhibitions.

(4) To report to the National Council the evidence taken, together with its findings and recommendations.

The Cinema Commission commenced its labours on January 8, 1917, and terminated on July 9, 1917. Forty-three witnesses were examined, representing the different interests in the country. In addition to the time taken up for the hearing of these witnesses, sittings were held at a private theatre for the inspection of the films complained of. It also extensively visited cinema halls in the course of its labours.

The headings for discussion were:—The standard of judgment, Special consideration regarding the cinema as a place of amusement, The moral dangers of darkness, The character of the film, Need of a stricter censorship, Special claims of children, Special inquiry regarding the influence of the picture house upon children, Juvenile crime, Replies of chief constables, Ideas of life and conduct, Special provision for the young, The value of the picture house, The cinema as a counter-attraction to the public-house.

The Commission also adopted the roll of educational expert, carrying out a number of psychological experiments.

(1) The durability of cinema impressions on school children;

(2) Mental fatigue caused by instruction by means of the cinema;

(3) Tests of education by cinematographical methods, in comparison with the ordinary method of instruction;

(4) In which direction the most fruitful and permanent results could be obtained by the cinema;

(5) The possibility of the cinema in cultivating an æsthetic appreciation;

(6) The most advantageous way of correlating the work of the school with that of the cinema, and the most economical method of using the cinema for this purpose;

(7) The collection of evidence with regard to experiments which have already been carried out effectively by using the cinema for educational purposes;

(8) The best methods of producing suitable films for school purposes.

This report is exhaustive and is the findings of laborous sittings, full of material treating upon the cinema question from all possible sides. The debates have been carried out by representatives of every section of the community; the decisions are unbiassed, full of truth, suggestions, and remedies.

Film Censorship

Owing to the objectionable character of some of the imported films, the question of an independent censorship was discussed at the latter end of 1911, and in October, 1912, with the approval of the Home Secretary, the Board of Censors was established and official duties were commenced in January, 1913. Entire independence and impartiality were assured, and are claimed to have been maintained by the Board of Censors.

It was decided to issue certificates classed as follows:—

U. Films to be shown to any audience.
A. Films to be shown to adults only.

This Board passes about 97 per cent. of films passing through its hands.

Two rules were laid down—

(1) That the living figure of Christ should not be allowed.

(2) That under no circumstances whatever would nudity be permitted.

The Examiners judged upon the broad principle that nothing should be passed which in their opinion would demoralize an audience. They laid down forty-three reasons for refusing to pass films.

The question is often asked in the public Press, and occasionally in Parliament, "What has become of the censor? Why does he not exercise his powers of suppression? Is there such an office?" This question is becoming increasingly urgent and acute.

There has been a tendency for the last two years to allow to filter through on to the public market films distasteful to modest vision. The so-called comic films are becoming more and more suggestive. We are aware that the modern tendency in female attire is to lower the neck and shorten the skirt. There is beauty in a painted nude figure, showing the perfect formation of limbs; this is from the standpoint of art.

It is the prevailing fashion in modern American "comedy films" for "bathing belles" to figure largely, and this is unnecessary unless the film actually depicts seaside life, surf-bathing, or is advertising a standard bathing costume approved of by the exponents of the "modiste" costume. There are also passages in these films which call for the excision of certain portions.

A flagrant breach of "censorship" is occasioned by allowing a film of the following nature to appear upon the open market. This depicts a Chinaman who runs an opium den, and who is also a money-lender. The story goes that he has designs upon a pretty English girl. To become acquainted, he advances money to her father, followed by further loans, which are used as a lever; for the father finally forces his pretty daughter to marry the Chinaman.

The scene changes to the girl's bedroom, where the pretty wife, clad in a diaphanous nightdress, has a terrific struggle with the Chinaman.

Only one conclusion is possible, and there is no moral attached to the picture, which only produces a feeling of disgust—that the paternal human nature should have been so shown as actually existing between father and daughter.

Juvenile Crime

Crime films are another section which should not escape the critical eye of the censor. It has been suggested that in some cases acts of crime by juveniles have been incited by seeing similar scenes enacted upon the screen. They have endeavoured to imitate and emulate the pictorial crime creator, who was lucky enough to evade the long arm of the law, by which they themselves were caught.

One cannot imagine for one moment that the display of films showing murder, suicide, arson, violence or theft, would leave a happy impression upon the human mind. It only fires the impressionable mind of the juvenile, who ultimately finds himself arraigned in the "juvenile court." Such films only injure the reputation of the cinemas exhibiting them, because sensible parents will forbid their children to enter such places.

The prevention of crime is depicted by a series of "Police pictures" in the Metropolis. This film, promoted to defend that great wall which defines the orderly and disorderly sections of the community, shows "Robert" (as he is lovingly called) in the discharge of his duties, which is not only to exercise a ceaseless vigilance, but to come into contact with danger of which many of us are ignorant.

It shows us the daily routine of every member of the police force, from the highest to the lowest rank. Scotland Yard is seen in all its specialized branches. One can see the detectives being trained to prevent and discover crime, and the manner in which they run social offenders to justice, and the deductions leading up to the trail.

The policeman is shown as a friend and helper to the young and aged, and children nowadays are taught to regard him as someone to appeal to in case they are lost, and not to run away at sight as if pursued by a spectre.

Morality Tests

A comprehensive attempt is being made in the United States to improve the quality of the films shown, and for this purpose a "National Motion Picture League" has been formed. It is proposed to elevate the standard in two ways—first by supervising and conducting children's matinées, and assisting churches, municipal boards of education, parents' associations and other organizations interested in public welfare to secure proper pictures for adults, young people and children. In the second place it will assist, by proper publicity, towards the provision of good pictures and a campaign of education against the immoral and objectionable ones.

A reviewing board has been formed by the League, composed of clergymen, Sunday school teachers and public welfare workers. This Board makes a selection from the general output of films, and a list of those which they deem suitable will be published in weekly bulletins before the pictures are released for the open market and public exhibition. These lists are sent to the film-producers, and are published in magazines. Local committees are formed everywhere to unite in their efforts and use every influence. These committees are of two kinds—children's matinées, which seek to provide suitable programmes for youthful minds; and reviewing committees, which report on all pictures seen in local picture theatres which are considered suitable for the lists of the League.

The films selected are clever and wholesome throughout. Films unsuitable, even though the details exercise the moral ending, are rigidly excluded. They have to be in good taste, unbiassed and accurate. The board refuses to endorse a film that is inaccurate from a scientific standpoint or that contains undesirable inaccuracies in the production of well-known stories.

No crimes are allowed in pictures if they show killing or gunplay, and there must also be no cruelty to either man or beast. Infidelity and sex pictures are not tolerated, and even scenes of women smoking or men drinking are debarred.

A rule has been instituted which would produce good in this country, and should be followed. All titles and letter-press must be strictly grammatical and free from profanity or vulgarity.

The following is a label on a film after having passed through their hands:—

"In part 3, cut out scenes of mixing drinks." In part 6 cut out sub-title, "You don't care a damn," etc., also all drinking scenes.

In short, the National Association of the Motion-Picture Industry has resolved to suppress and refrain from films that "emphasize vice or the sex appeal or illicit love; exhibit nudity, excessive demonstrations of passion, and vulgar postures; unduly concern themselves with the underworld of crime, bloodshed and violence, drunkenness, gambling, and unnatural practices; emphasize the methods used in committing crime; bring into ridicule the law, the authorities, and religious beliefs and leaders; contain salacious titles, or are advertised salaciously."

The "White Scourge" Problem

The "white slave traffic" is as much a scourge as tuberculosis. This appalling problem is sapping the vitality of the nation, and every means of giving publicity to this menace, which, unfortunately, is not on the wane, should be used. We have the best possible publicity agent in the film. Such a film could be prepared and exhibited to initiate the ignorant, and to show those who practise in it that something is being done openly to expose this illicit traffic.

One reads in the newspapers almost daily of wrecked lives, fathers who have shot their daughters and then themselves, because she has trodden the downward path; and of others who have made away with themselves because they are beyond reclamation.

This subject is talked about, and often whispered, as if it were a plague and they were afraid of becoming infected with it.

It is a plague, and requires to be stamped out, like the Plague of London.

The daily life of the unfortunate daughter of the streets and her means of livelihood could not be portrayed more eloquently. The efforts of the reclaimer of lost souls would be strengthened. Mothers would give silent prayers for the imparting of such information to their daughters, which, although their duty, it is often shunned, to the detriment of her offspring.

In a clean, inoffensive and simple way it could be shown how unfortunate girls, attracted by finery and dress, are sometimes directly led into these channels.

If the book entitled "The Rise and Fall of Susan Lennox" could be suitably filmed, then much would have been accomplished in this direction.

Mrs. Caudle's "Curtain Lectures" would not be needed at home. The impression upon the young mind would be indelible. The voiceless foster-mother would repeat the lesson to thousands of young people.

The allied question "venereal disease" has already appeared upon the screen and thousands have already benefited by it. The Manchester Corporation has taken steps to give publicity by means of the film, and if the idea is generally approved and encouraged, much will be done to educate citizens of the dangers of this malignant disease. Let us hope that greater efforts will be made to bring these evils home.

Churches and the Cinema

Now that ministers are bemoaning the smallness of their congregations, and declaring that the flock has gone astray, wondering how to account for the fact that modern-day religious opinions have changed, and in some cases, warped; that they no longer come to hear good sermons and music, that the collections are mean; that their social functions are unattended—they ask themselves, "What is wrong, and what is the remedy?"

The cinema has been tried in the church to evoke that enthusiasm now dormant. In America it has met with huge success and is being recommended by the clerical body throughout that country as a means of reviving lost interest. Ministers' sermons have brought to life the actual characters; there seems to be a new atmosphere within the sacred precincts, and the churches are not large enough to hold the congregations. The sermons are more lucidly expounded, the attention of the congregation is held, no stentorian snores reverberate through the church, there is no coughing or impatient moving of feet or imperfect sneezing; and even the child with its contribution in its pocket keeps it there without dropping it on the floor. Such rapt attention has been evoked by the film entitled "Creation." This Italian production presents the history of the Old Testament in pictorial form. The film begins with Creation and closes with the reign of King Solomon, the total length is 30,000 feet, and it is in twenty-two chapters.

Could one see a more realistic film than the actual creation of the world, the birth of Christ in the manger, His movements amongst the people, the healing of the sick, the restoration of sight to the blind, the lame made to walk, His successes and failures, His friends and His enemies, and the conversion of His disciples, His last supper, crucifixion and final resurrection?

No minister need appeal for a more stirring picture, a better demonstration than this; his sermons would be more explicit and better understood. Films could be created to suit every sermon, or sermons could be worded to suit the picture chosen, and to one versed in theology, notes would be unnecessary. Enthusiasm would grip the preacher as the film rolled on, and words would come easily and spontaneously.

A new picture just "released" in Sweden would do well in this direction, the title of which is "Thy soul shall bear witness." It is a sermon in pictures, more graphically described than by any pen; and is beautifully told and accurately expressed.

The story is of an outcast waiting in a graveyard for the New Year to dawn, in order that he and his comrades may drink a curse to the months that are to come. A young social worker on her deathbed is calling for him, but he ignores the call. Even his friends are disgusted with his behaviour as he tells them the legend of the cart of death which drives everywhere and collects the souls of the dead, the driver being the man who has died on New Year's Day. He falls under the spell of a social worker who battles to save his soul, and to restore him to his constant and faithful wife. He finally awakens, to find it a horrible dream and that he has slept in the churchyard. Other items enter the story, but the impression left behind remains, leaving the moral intended.

The Film and the Savage

One would hardly think that the film has reached and is being used in some of the remotest corners of the globe, yet such is the case. The advance made in this direction of the education of these savages by means of the film has been a source of help to the missionaries. These natives, quick-witted, are apt to learn far quicker from motion pictures than from personal instruction. The effects are sometimes very humorous, imitation is often indulged in, and bobbed hair and short skirts have created such an impression that the fashion prevails as far away as Jamaica. The black belle "bobs" her hair and even covers her skin with a pearl powder overlaid with rouge and a peculiar dark red in imitation of her Western sister.

She tucks in her print skirt, and if she is accustomed to going barefooted during the week, on Sunday she will appear in vivid silk stockings. She wears a hat woven by herself, with a twisted impressionistic scarf such as the heroine in a screen play wears when she sallies forth to meet her hero. It is contended that there is already a marked improvement in the manners and customs, which schools have not been able to bring about.

There is ample scope for pioneer work amongst these dusky brethren, and the projector would go a long way towards attaining this end.

Co-operative Cinemas

Mr. George Bernard Shaw says, "There is no reason why cinema theatres should not be added to the list of public wants provided for by the co-operative movement." Certainly the Co-operative Society have their interests in nearly every concern going. For the instruction of their members, physically and mentally, they have made every endeavour to fill in the gaps. If their energies were also turned to the establishment of cinemas for educational purposes, including instructional and wholesome films, then co-operators will have made a forward movement.

V
COMMERCIAL ADVERTISING

Advertising by the Film

As an advertising medium the film stands unrivalled, and, probably, in time to come, it will supplant the flaring posters so distasteful to our vision, and which disfigure and desecrate our landscapes.

Various manufacturing firms could further avail themselves of this latest product of visual exhibition. Manufacturers of gas mantles could demonstrate the whole process of the manufacture of these flimsy yet durable illuminators, from the extracting of the fibre to the finished article, the candle powers of each, and what they are used for.

Again, an opportunity occurs for the Ediswan, Mazda, Tantalum and other electric bulb manufacturers to represent the blowing of the glass and the fixing of the sensitive filaments which convey the electric current and produce cheap illumination.

British and colonial railways have found the cinema a good substitute for the glaring advertisements in their endeavours to lure the holiday-makers to the beauty and health spots served by their train systems. This method of advertising would speak more than volumes and be more vividly impressed upon the minds of the audience than by many an hour of searching through railway and holiday guides, or touring announcements.

Visualize a trip on one of the railways—say, passing through impressive mountainous scenery. As each station is passed and the journey progresses, bird's-eye views could be shown of fruitful and restful country never seen before, and sometimes it would help to influence a holiday-maker who is contemplating where to go for his next holiday.

The Continent could be advertised upon the screen by companies conducting tours. We should see Parisian life as it is lived, the boulevards and cafes, and everywhere the places of national importance. The architecture of our towns is too often deplorable, and in contrast to that seen in towns like Hamburg, Frankfort, Brussels or Milan, not to mention the great capitals and the cities of historic beauty and significance like Florence, Venice and

Nuremburg; these majestic structures would appeal to all lovers of the finer arts.

The prejudiced and those behind the times may argue that the "pictures" are suited only to the illiterate. But, judge the cinema as our minds dictate, the fact remains that this new vitalizing force has entered into the educational progress of to-day.

Sales by the Film

Keen competition in manufactured articles has brought about increasing difficulties in the sales of machinery. The manufacturer has learned, by sad experience, that it is sometimes impossible to convince his prospective customer of the superiority of his product over that of a rival firm, without actual inspection. Size prevents him from carrying his machine to the customer, and distance will not permit the customer to go to the machine. In this dilemma the progressive manufacturer has joyfully hailed the advent of the motion picture film which enables him to display every step in the manufacture of the machine or articles, and every phase of its operation.

When the maker of machinery, plants, and equipment asks the average person to look over blue prints and written descriptions, and thus form a conclusion as to the worth of his products, he usually finds himself in a difficulty. It is mentally impossible for the general run of people to visualize or imagine a plant or machinery in working and running order from an inspection of drawings and written descriptions, no matter how graphic or conclusive they may be.

Machines are generally too large to be shipped around for inspection by the prospective customer. It is physically impossible to ship all plants and processes, and very frequently the prospective purchaser cannot arrange to visit a place where machinery can be inspected. The modern motion projector is light in weight, small in size, and can be easily operated. Films can be shown at any place, at any time, and are the ideal method of demonstrating the salesman's wares. Some manufacturers are making a speciality of these portable projectors, which may be tapped to the lighting circuit and used in the office of the prospective customer, with a blank wall as a screen.

This method of exhibition has been hailed with delight, and the number of manufacturers availing themselves of this medium of salesmanship grows in number day by day.

VI
PRODUCTION

One writer gloomily said, recently, that every cinema was in a bad way, and inferred that the films were a failure; the distressing shrinkage of the audiences signified the general non-approval of the tone of the films submitted. It is not that the people have not the money; in spite of the stress of the times, cinema theatres are the best patronized places of amusement, and the fact that these companies are paying a dividend (anything from seventy-five to ninety per cent.), spells, in one word, "success," which means a good turnover and good profits.

The Failure and Success of the Film

I do agree in this respect, that the British public is becoming much more critical, and in time will insist that it get its value, or else will steer clear of the cinemas. It is for the managership to provide the films with the necessary tone. There are several factors governing this criticism and decline, and one is that the English film production started with an unsound foundation, or a bad tradition. Give a dog a bad name and it will stick to it, and to retrieve a lost reputation is a difficult feat, yet not an impossible one.

If the British producers were composed of Englishmen alone, and not a conglomeration of nationalities, the plots in the various novels and plays would be produced exactly as intended and not murdered and warped as at the present time. To read the book, then see the play, and finally the film, one is astonished at the vast difference in the rendering; the whole plot being considerably changed.

The rendering of the film should be exactly the same as the play, and as one reads, yet it is widely different. It is either "cut" or lengthened; the important is ignored and the unimportant is enlarged upon, showing in striking features the blunders perpetrated. What is the result of this doctoring? Instead of the producers raking in the thousands and pleasing millions of patrons, the whole production is a miserable failure, and the reputation of the author as a writer is belittled in the eyes of the public.

To prevent this, the producers could approach the author to supervise the production and pay him a nominal retaining fee, and the public would

be assured of an exact reproduction of the play or plot they have seen acte
and wish to see filmed.

In film production the British would create an improvement in the films if some of the American methods were copied. It is the latter custom to secure the presence of the author throughout the whole perio of production, and his critical judgment and suggestions ensure the exa reproduction of the film as written.

All films are not a failure, far from it. Several British films have bee excellently produced, and the plot has remained as originally written. Th is what the reading public requires and looks for, especially when they ar familiar with the story. The exact reproduction of the plot without alteratio does much to secure the confidence of the patrons.

At the present time the British film-producers are handicapped b the American film-tax, which reduces considerably the scope of sale, bu if only out of fairness to this country the tax should be dropped—or ou Government must perforce raise a similar barrier to protect British produce in this country.

The prospects for British producers are brighter, and if they can exhib at the various "Trade Shows" films worth seeing—from the standpoint c acting, scenario and production—then they need not fear a "block" in th bookings for English films.

The British public is patriotic, and it only remains for the Britis producers to bring out something really good for foreign competition t fall behind. Our keenest competitors are America, Germany, Italy an Switzerland.

Cinema Eccentricities: Blunders and Inaccuracies

Some remarkable blunders are perpetrated in the production of som modern films, either due to an oversight on the part of the producer wh endeavours to make it too realistic, or inattention to details. These incident have a tendency to do more harm to the cinema than good, for these littl slips which have been allowed to creep in and appear on the screen are apt t make the picture patrons become impatient. Some people find amusemen in the noting of all these blunders. Let me enumerate a few to show what mean, for they are too apparent to escape notice. For instance—

A monk in a picture of the twelfth century is seen to switch off th electric light!

Louis the XIVth is supposed to remark to a lady-in-waiting, that she wants "taking down a peg," an expression not quite in keeping with the period portrayed!

Again, it is just as ridiculous for vaccination marks to be shown on the left arm of a harem-queen of the East—period, a thousand years ago!

One sees such items as, a view of Curzon Street, showing huge pillared porticoes and palms.

A duke who wears appalling American "reach-me-downs."

A duchess who is Irish, and therefore must say "Be jabers" and "Begorra."

Views of English countryside and ducal park, displaying granite boulders, tropical palms and scores of American cars all on the wrong side of the road!

Another delightful oversight—a man who enters a strip of undergrowth wearing a tie, walks straight through and emerges with an up-to-date West End made-up bow, to the old miser in "Wuthering Heights"; the times are Victorian, and a conspicuous object is a safe made in 1915.

One laughs at the absurdity of the whole thing, when a lady in a crinoline is shown knitting a jumper; or a disreputable attic is furnished with a beautifully carved wooden bed, fitted with silken hangings.

Copies of the "Peerage" figure in this satire—of course it is American—and it is such instances which are creating a bad name for the cinema. American ignorance of the British peerage is shown in the film featuring an old Warwickshire family, Armitage by name; a beautiful daughter, the Honourable Diana Gwen Beaufort, etc., Armitage. Her young brother remained the plain unvarnished "Eddie"; her mother "Mrs. Armitage," and they were apparently not on the same aristocratic level as the Hon. Gwen. A framed copy of the family crest is much to the fore. It is only too noticeable that the Hon. Gwendoline is in direct succession to the family honours, totally excluding her living brother. In the end this captivating young personage marries an ordinary American commoner; the honeymoon is spent at the ancestral home in Warwickshire—Armitage Castle. How, or why she got there the film story does not relate.

Such ignorance causes the public to distrust all films, and does much to lessen the attendance of intelligent people at the cinema theatres.

Natural Colour Films

Most film pictures shown upon the screen are at present of the black and white variety, and colour films are sometimes spoken of as being generally impracticable. The main item which is the cause of the non-general appearance of these films in natural colour is the question of cost. Experiments have been highly successful, but the necessary standard of apparatus has to be secured to produce the colours of nature in reality, and this is the reason why natural colour films have been slow in receiving commercial recognition. The items entering into consideration are—extra equipment and extra help.

A colour-film has to be very realistic, and to secure its real market value its ascendancy over the ordinary black and white film has to be proved. If the "projector" required it to be elaborate, the stage effects to be in unison, its chances as a commercial venture are greatly reduced on account of the high cost of film rental. The various expensive processes of production have greatly retarded its progress—hence its rarity.

Colour films are usually accepted as natural colour films, whereas, in reality, natural colour sometimes does not exist. A great number of these natural colour films are hand painted, mostly produced in France, where this subtle art of colour deception is practised to advantage. Films are tastefully and artistically coloured, requiring excessive patience and skill from hundreds of workers; for it is no easy task to paint these miniatures, measuring one inch by three-quarters of an inch.

This process of painting is carried out by stages. One scene is gone through, taking a single character—a house, background or foliage in its various shades. The process is tedious and there lurks the ever-present danger of making mistakes which would spoil the whole effect.

Photography plays an important part in the reproduction in natural colours, and the fact that dyes and chemicals can be used for this purpose is overlooked by many people—red, orange, green, yellow, violet and blue, when mixed in varying degrees, produce any shade known to the human eye.

The earliest attempt at a natural colour process for the film was made in 1907; the combined efforts and experiments of an Englishman and an American. Their efforts were very successful, the pictures being particularly clear and realistic. An improved process has been developed which reproduces objects, whether stationary or in motion, bringing forth the natural colours to be found in nature at her best.

It is to be regretted that the colour films cannot be cheapened in the process of production, for nothing delights the hearts of patrons more than to see before their eyes scenes and places with which they are familiar; every object of still life (plants), or the living animals roaming amidst their natural-coloured surroundings.

Talking Films

The talking picture commenced its venture, fettered. It was introduced to the public whilst in its infancy; experiments had been few, hence these two combining factors failed to work in harmony, and consequently faith in its future progress was badly shattered.

The leading difficulty was the question of synchronising the sound and pictures, for to speak accurately they must be in perfect step. The simplest talking film is the combination of an ordinary phonograph and a projector. The phonograph placed near the actors registers the sounds whilst the camera records the action.

In the question of synchronism lies the difference of the various schemes promoted in the past; the two main essentials must be kept in unison, otherwise the whole thing becomes a farce. Intricate time-arrangements, synchronized motors, loud-speaking telephone arrangements have yielded but poor results. One attempt was tried whereby the film carried the sound record along one edge side by side with the pictures. A stylus is made to travel in a groove on the film, and apparently synchronization is complete, but the test results turned out anything but satisfactory.

For recording sounds or speech, sensitive microphones are distributed about the scene where the play is being acted. These microphones are skilfully concealed, in a fern or palm, underneath a desk or table, anywhere so that it is skilfully camouflaged from the vision of the actors taking part. The sound waves impinging on the microphones are transferred to a circuit including a battery and a string-galvanometer, highly sensitive; the string attached to this galvanometer is hung over a series of very powerful electro-magnets, and the slightest fluctuations in the current passing through it causes an immediate distortion. Powerful arc lamps are mounted at the rear of the camera and a beam of light penetrates through the galvanometer, throwing a shadow of the wire on a steadily moving film behind a narrow horizontal slip. The wire is so arranged that one side of the exposed film is always in the shadow, the developed film shows a straight edge and a series of mountain tops, or peaks.

The galvanometer is the heart of the sound recorder. A single wire was employed in the earlier forms. An oil bath is provided through which the upper part of the wire passes, which damps the movement. This instrument can be easily opened; provision also being made for adjusting the wire best suited for the sound record.

The reproducing process is easy. A fine telephonic relay, highly sensitive, is employed in circuit with the selenium cell and battery, in addition, a clear-speaking telephone with its own battery is operated in the secondary circuit. The second record of the film is transmitted into sound waves, which are generated throughout the cinema at the same time the pictures are being shown on the screen.

Quite recently in London a new process was shown, comprising a transmitter, electrically connected by means of an ordinary telephone wire to the reproducing instruments, which are placed in the frame of the screen, and a double turntable carries the musical records, which are automatically controlled by the film in such a way that the change from one record to another is made without pause or hesitancy, and in absolute conjunction with the movement of the pictures. An outstanding feature is that the apparatus can be easily connected with any existing cinema projector.

Speaking-films of short duration are a great attraction and fairly successful to undertake, but their real value as an effective synchronizer would be fairly tested reel film. The obstacles to be overcome here would be tremendous; it would mean constant rehearsing, over and over again, until the players were absolutely perfect in word as well as in action, and the excision of any part of the film would interfere with the reproduction.

Accidents sometimes happen to films, such as tearing, firing, severe scratching, and this necessitates the cutting away of part of the film. This possibility of interruption is minimized in the new apparatus; the operator can adjust the gramophone to make allowance for the cutting off of one or two feet of film, but not beyond this extent. Lecturers find the film not altogether satisfactory to aid them in demonstrating their lectures; the drawback lies in the fact that he sometimes wishes to stop the film to emphasize some particular passages in his lecture, but a new process has now come to his aid which will relieve him of this anxiety. The film is passed through a water jacket, which is attached to the projecting machine, and this enables film to be stopped at any point, for any length of time. This experiment has been made with current ranging from 30 to 60 amperes, and even at 60 it has been found possible to maintain the film stationary for ten minutes.

Take Professor Stirling's lecture. A Gallic cock is thrown upon a screen, life-like in its pride and colours; it ruffled its feathers and inflated its gorge, and opened its beak, then there came forth the most strident and triumphant cock-crows ever heard at dawn; and so perfectly did the sounds correspond to the actions of the bird, that it was almost impossible to believe that the real bird was not there.

After experiments extending over ten years, a Swedish engineer, M. Sven Berglund, has succeeded in inventing a speaking film, which ensures the simultaneous production of sound and action. Upon the heel of this invention comes another by an Englishman; the perfect voice-movement film having reached a definite advanced stage. The invention of a synchronizer by Mr. Claude H. Verity, a Harrogate engineer, enables the operator, by simply sliding a knob, quite independently of observing the screen, to work synchronization to 1-24th of a second. For operas with singing and music, a child could operate it because there is a fixed tempo. Should the film break by accident, the speaking can be shut off and taken up again. A great advantage of the invention is that with the apparatus in projecting boxes the synchronized film could be circulated in the ordinary way.

Still another invention by an Englishman, which goes a long way towards the perfection of these pictures, is one by which the pictures are made sharper and deeper in tone, besides being steadier; this is done by a series of mirrors. It has often been noticed that some of the pictures when thrown upon the screen lack "body," or shall we call it "substance"? By this means the pictures are made more realistic than ever; the natural lines on the human face are visible, so life-like and human do they appear.

Screen improvements are also taking place. The new Ekualite diminishes the amount of eyestrain, and the front benchers may watch pictures without that periodical resting from the concentrated gaze. It ensures perfect comfort of vision from any angle of a cinema hall.

It is needless to point out that the extension of the idea is possible, the application of the cinematograph and chronophone are illimitable, and how much more will the Library lectures and "Half-hour talks" be appreciated! Hundreds of years hence, our descendants may see and hear their forefathers as if their living ghosts talked and walked, long after their bones have become dust.

Paper Films

British ingenuity and invention has produced a further revolution in film production, reducing cost and minimizing fire risks. The inventor of this innovation in paper photoplay is Mr. Martin Harper, of London, who also has the credit to his name of producing the "Extralite" flickerless shutter. The commercial samples have been described as "everything the inventor claims for them."

These paper films will not blacken or singe, which claim has been proved by subjecting them to the excessive heat generated by the projector, and they are absolutely non-inflammable. There is also an additional valu to these films, when shown on the screen: they produce wonderful picture soft in tone, with more body than the celluloid films. These films wi withstand wear and tear, the "jumping" of the film caused by vibration du to a well-worn film will be eliminated.

Other advantages derived from the appearance of the paper film ar that the cost of production is claimed to be only one-tenth of the celluloi film. Lighting cost of projection is reduced by one-third, and the price c the projector, which is simple in construction in comparison with th complicated lens system, costs considerably less.

The outcome is obvious, and there is every possibility of the film and th projector being introduced into the home for amusement and entertainmer during family gatherings at a Christmas treat, etc. Some people hav actually had films prepared of the gambols of their own children, which i later years will be shown to them as "what they used to be in childhood. This idea will undoubtedly grow now that the paper film has appeared an proved its durability.

Paper films will affect a whole number of concerns. Cinema-operatin rooms need not be asbestos-lined to conform with fire-insurance policie cost of construction will be easier and cheaper, and insurance rates wi be lower. The operator also will be relieved of that ceaseless vigilance s necessary with a celluloid film.

The existing bye-laws now governing film exhibitions under th Cinematograph Act will be questioned. This Act only covers celluloid film these printed paper slips are neither films nor celluloid.

All this reduced cost of purchase and maintenance will commend itse to private enterprises and manufacturers generally. Greater possibilities ar foreshadowed in being able to demonstrate the efficiency of their finishe articles.

The general use of the cinema in the schools has been "tabooed" i some quarters on account of the fire possibilities. This difficulty has no been overcome, so that one may see in the near future this voiceless teache working and instructing the scholars.

Much more could have been said dealing with technicalities—suc as the construction of the camera, editing, acting, trick photography an supposed realities; spirit photographs, cartoons becoming animated wit life, and moving sculpture—but these must be left to the imaginative min of the critic.

VII
CONCLUSION

Upon reflection, the effect produced by the cinematograph upon our lives and thoughts, nay, upon the nation as a whole, must be considerable—morally, physically, spiritually, mentally and psychologically, for this form of amusement absorbs part of the daily thoughts of a considerable percentage of the British public. The reaction upon the mind becomes apparent from the quality of the subject-matter shown. There are certain members of the community who stand apart from this form of occupation of their leisure moments. This lack of moral courage, of the possibility of becoming tainted with the lower tone of some of the pictures, is to be deplored. Let social workers and educationists view the films and judge for themselves; and decry those films which, in their opinion, are unfit for mental consumption.

The greatest service can be rendered to humanity if the cinematograph be used in the right direction. There is a crying need for more educational films. This progression is retarded because production, at the present time, is centralized. This centralization, as we all well know, takes place in America, but before long there will be a breakaway, and British producers will think for themselves and not be influenced by Americanism.

The population of England and America is widely different. The American population is self-supporting, providing vast fields for opportunities, and these opportunities are considerably helped by prevailing climatic conditions. In England, production is periodical, governed by climatic conditions; in America, in California, the weather conditions are ideal and consistent. The two governing factors are at hand—financial support, and the weather.

British productions have soared above the fourth-raters, and the standard has undoubtedly risen during the last few years. The recent cry of one British Colony to the producers in this country was—"Send us more British films."

As stated before, and voiced by the powerful press, a more discriminating censorship is required. If these duties were carried out more rigidly by an authorised person capable of giving an unbiassed judgment, not only on questionable films, but from the standpoint of national character, such discretion would exercise the necessary restraining guidance.

The Government subsidizes the dye industry, and why should not the educational side of the film industry receive the same consideration? This would produce "standardized educational films," and might lead to good results.

The cinema question is uppermost in the mind of the public, and every phase is looked to with interest, every new invention eagerly investigated, and every suggestion for the raising of the masses, both morally and mentally, is given a whole-hearted support. It is hoped that although there may be passages in this volume with which readers will not "see eye to eye," these pages will have been read with interest; and will help educationists to realize more fully the great power that the film may become in the education of the people.